SOME RHYMES, ⹁⹁

Gilly O'Brien

ARTHUR H. STOCKWELL LTD
Torrs Park   Ilfracombe   Devon
Established 1898
www.ahstockwell.co.uk

British Library Cataloguing-in-Publication Data.
A catalogue record for this book is available
from the British Library.

ISBN 978-0-7223-3934-3
Printed in Great Britain by
Arthur H. Stockwell Ltd
Torrs Park   Ilfracombe
Devon

Contents

BORN LUCKY

Two sisters,
Two sons:

Great family
All as one.

Huge on hearts,
Big on brains;

Hard workers
Bring the gains.

Black cat,
Lucky charms,

Fill our home,
Adorn the arms.

Laugh with friends
All year through,

Always willing
To try something new.

The cheeky one,
Mother once said.

No, the lucky one
With the words in her head.

TOO SUDDEN

Still in shock:
Where have you gone?
It was all so quick,
Even the legal work's done.

The house is empty,
The carpets are swept,
Ready for new people –
And oh, how we've wept!

Clearing your room,
Finding treasures aplenty,
Discovering your lifetime
Boxes filled equals twenty.

At the start of '08
You were still here;
Now halfway through
You've joined Mother dear.

Miss you so much, Pa,
But feel you're around.
Long to hug and talk,
But silence is the sound.

HEAVENLY PICTURE

I spotted the picture of you –
It was in a sacred place.
Others may not have noticed,
But I saw such a happy face.

Was that your sanctuary?
Did the people make you smile?
Or was it the surroundings –
A chance to get away for a while?

You looked so at home there.
I felt like that once too
With like-minded friends
Together and smiling through.

What a great big grin!
It was a photo I had never seen.
Strange that there are probably more,
Now remaining just a dream.

Only you knew the reason why,
But I think I have guessed.
And may you be in peace now –
You certainly are blessed.

ALL WRONG

They have no future;
They had some past;
They only have today.
For how long it will last?

There'll be no happy ending,
For he'll always belong to *her*.
It's rapidly drifting apart.
Go back to how you were.

As much as they try and try
They'll never be truly free,
For there is so much to deal with.
It was never meant to be.

Blessed with a love and lust
That could have lasted for ever –
Wrong time, wrong place, wrong person –
Their lives entwined. No, never!

MEL'S MOVE

Sometimes I wish I didn't love you so much.
Things never go to plan.
I only wanted to dance with you
And talk to a charismatic man.

If I had known it would take us this far,
I might never have opened my mouth,
For you are living up North
And I am here in the South.

There are miles and miles between us,
The hours turn into days.
It would be good to meet more often,
But that's rarer than sun's rays.

So where do we go from here –
Rewind, fast forward or stay?
You are free in the evenings,
And I am free during the day.

To stay as we are is too painful;
To quit would be quite a task.
Time to change our situation –
I dread having to ask.

GROWING OLD

Who will kiss me now you are gone?
It's all too much to bear.

I am no longer fit and young,
But I still need your loving care.

Who will hug me now you are gone?
Everything is such a muddle.

I am no longer fit and young,
But I still need your cuddle.

Who will share my secrets now you are gone?
I have too many fears.

I am no longer fit and young,
But still need you to wipe the tears.

Who will have my heart now you are gone?
It's nearly broken in two.

I am no longer fit and young,
But I still need to be with you.

BETTER NOW

When you are with me
I feel no pain.

With you beside me
There is no rain.

Walking together
Alone in the sun,

Laughing out loud,
Having so much fun.

The winter is here,
But I am not cold.

Where once I was shy
You make me feel bold.

You drive me on to paths
I'd never normally find.

Where once I was angry
You made me so kind.

I never saw
Before you came along

That I was so lost,
So I've written this song.

Freedom of a new life –
So welcome and cautious.

Big steps all round –
No time to be nervous.

Run with the job;
Turn a different corner.

The future is brighter and
Very much warmer.

HURT

Stick, stone,
Skin and bone
Battered and bruised today.

Don't shout;
Please hug
And then be on your way.

Find someone else,
Or, even better,
Have no one at all.

Calm down,
Put fist in pocket,
Go shout at the wall.

CONTACT

No word,
No call,
No text
At all.

Not a sign,
Not a note.
If only
He wrote.

That's it, huh?
So sad to say
No contact then
Call it a day.

He moved on,
She stayed still –
Tough on her!
Hurt it will.

BUSY LIVES

You there,
She here –
Why?

You can meet,
She can call –
When?

Drive up,
Train down –
Where?

Easy really,
But too hard –
What?

Grab an hour,
Snatch a kiss –
How?

See less,
Fit in more.
Now?

DEAR MUMMY

Thank you for the memories
Stored in my head.
Thank you for your old books –
The best I have read.

Thank you for the love
Filling my heart,
Thank you for the hug –
It was so hard to part.

Thank you for the guidance –
You always feel so near.
Thank you for your faith,
Which you held so dear.

Thank you for the wisdom
Needed wherever I go.
Thank you for being there,
But now I miss you so.

ROLLER-COASTER LIFESTYLE

For how long
Will it be like this –

Either down in the dumps
Or living in bliss?

Who is responsible?
Who has the power to change?

Is it just one source
Or part of a range?

Let go of one dream
To resume another.

Keep changing your mind –
So like her brother.

Why go through it?
You wear them all out.

Have a normal life –
Put paid to all the doubt.

HELP

Such a sad office:
Grey and tired faces
No longer thriving,
All longing to change places.

Hold 1-2-1 sessions:
Listen to their moans,
Hear their ambitions,
Take an interest in the groans.

Scoop up the complaints –
Clients top the pile –
Make promises you will keep,
Go the extra mile.

Look at what you can change
Without discarding the best.
Chip away at each area –
Remember to savour the test.

Help inspire the business,
Put back the colour,
Give them pride and respect
Along with profit and valour.

OLIVE BRANCH

At least you turned up.
Such a sad thing to see:
It was all very hard,
But still she blanked he.

It was all very quiet –
Nothing left to say.
He stayed in the kitchen;
He felt in the way.

Yet this was his home
And you were the guest.
Couldn't do any more
And it was his best.

The olive branch given
And yet again ignored –
What more can he do,
So unadored?

SHE TRIED

She tried to love.
It was the only way she knew.

She tried to care for him,
But what more could she do?

She tried to nurse him
As much as she could.

She tried to support him
The way she felt she should.

Her way didn't suit him,
Either day or night.

She hopes he'll find another –
One who will get it right.

GAP YEARS

There's a vacuum in our lives,
Or is it the empty nest?

Is it time to do more things,
Or sit and have a rest?

Too old for a new child,
Too aged to change career.

Feels like we've retired early –
Too young to be an old dear.

So what is the solution?
Would a lover wear us out?

Time for new friends and pastimes:
Just have to get out and about.

CONFUSED

You are in her world –
Move along.

You are under her skin –
Go away.

You are in her head –
Get out.

You are needed –
Pause here.

You are her drive –
Carry on.

You are in her heart –
Stick around.

MUMS AND MOTORS

Such a dilemma:
Is it easy to park?
Fab chrome dashboard,
But the interior's too dark.

Is it eco-friendly?
Not fans of air-con –
Plenty of mirrors, though,
To put make-up on.

Two-seaters are preferable,
But there's no room for three kids.
Any type of wheels
Enough to control skids.

Like the bag and the shoes,
Want it in red and want it now.
Not worried about engine size –
Just something with a wow!

If I made my mind up,
Can we drive home today?
Taxed, insured and MOT'd –
Be great on the driveway.

INCONSOLABLE

She could not see to type.
The tears were flooding her face,
But the words flowed and flowed.
She was in a lonely place.

Her fingers were tapping quickly,
She was wailing as she worked,
The noise louder and louder –
It's funny how she coped.

Her sobs were racking her body,
Her shoulders ached with woe.
Tumbling out faster and faster,
The script was ready to go.

So broken was her heart.
Something else was driving –
She felt it nearer and nearer –
The reality and the feeling.

LIVING THE DREAM

Is the grass greener
On the other side?
Is real grass over there
Or just a place to hide?

Why have you gone there?
Was it just for the sun?
You found a job so quickly –
Such a lucky one.

Are you homesick yet?
Is the money running out?
Plenty of new friends surround you,
And much drinking about.

Come home, friend, we miss you.
Your quality of life has gone.
You watch the same programmes.
Your language course is done.

Only a couple of hours away:
The shopping is no better,
Your health is in decline,
The rain is no wetter.

Pop back now and again.
Dream on and you will find
Good times can still be had –
The English-speaking kind.

NICE TRY

From what point did it die?
At least she gave it a try.

Paid her way, did as asked,
Obeyed fully to whatever the task.

Definitely short on romance,
Bordering on boredom.

Feeling so foolish
For being the keen one.

Lack of emotion:
Was that down to he?

Obviously not keen,
Or too busy for she.

Used when vulnerable –
Is that how it feels?

Hard for her
To be one of your girls.

LOOKING FOR ME?

Feel my presence,
But don't look for me.
It's better you don't know
Where I am, where I go.

You have been sheltered
To soften the pain.
I am out there somewhere.
Believe and stop looking.

You feel me near
And I see your tears.
It's better you don't know
Where I am, where I go.

Watch for the rainbow –
Stars too, if you wish.
My love surrounds you
In whatever you do.

Try to work through it.
Time will surely heal.
It's better you don't know
Where I am, where I go.

You are safe now.
Have faith and start living.
Please, smile again.
I am watching over you.

It's better you don't know
Where I am, where I go.

GOING SOLO

Please, leave me
Alone for a while.

I need a chance
To laugh and smile.

The love we had
Is still around,

But I need my feet
Back on the ground.

I cannot start again,
Tired and weary.

My head aches,
My eyes are teary.

Go away, please,
But come back another time.

Yes, I still really
Want you to be mine.

PARTIED OUT

At least we've experienced it
And have the memories too.
Pity others that missed out –
    They had things to do.

The 'disco' generation
Looking back on happy times:
Such colourful places
And now part of these rhymes.

Not a worry in the world!
We've had such crazy fun
And laughed until we cried.
There was nothing else to be done.

So, best friend, we captured
Those days at the right era.
Photos of all-night partying
Now make you feel much nearer.

ETERNAL BACHELORS

Ring when it suits you –
Too busy to take a call,

You seem to think of nothing
Except work and football.

Always in the bar.
Are you so naive to think

That you are attractive
When so full of drink.

Can't take responsibility,
Spend money on your toys:

You never think of others,
Just act like little boys.

Scared of being domestic,
Shy away from family life

Until you need looking after.
Then start looking for a wife.

Is there any point?
You'll be bored and moving on.

The solo life a-calling,
And you'll be up and gone.

PET PATTER

Hello there, little one.
You are lively today.
Were you waiting for me
To come out and play?

You are not so young.
It's hard for you to walk,
But the noises you make –
Sounds like you talk.

Always there for a biscuit –
Lunch and supper too.
Your fur is white,
Your eyes are blue.

A faithful friend,
A loyal pal;
You adore your mistress –
She's quite a gal.

So very loving,
You are a treasure:
A true family dog
Giving so much pleasure.

N.Y.C.

Now you can see
What it is to be alone,

What it feels like to be poor,
What it is to be shown the door.

Now you can see,
When away from home,

That it is no joy or fun
To be alone in the sun.

Now you can see
How to struggle with life.

That you find your friends are
Not always at the bar.

Now you can see
The problems it brings

That you cannot think
Or work if you drink.

Now you can see
How hard it is

And how much it cost,
Look at what you have lost.

THEY WERE RIGHT

They were more than worried.
Are you sure you can do this?
It will take more than new trainers.
Here's a good-luck kiss.

She knew she was not fit enough;
She didn't run to win the race.
She knew she would finish
To wipe the smirk from that man's face.

So there you are at the start,
A number on your chest,
With every breath and intention
Of not stopping to take a rest.

You look around to see
So many brave and proud,
Running in all conditions,
Being cheered on by the crowd.

Arrive battered but a finisher
And the medal is shining new.
Oh, what an achievement!
And a dream come true.

OUT

The house was empty,
But nothing's changed.

Up the path to the gate –
But it was open.

He never tried to stop her,
But he could have.

Walk away to a new start,
But a strange one.

It's hard and it hurts,
But this is best for them.

They drove her there,
But the car wasn't needed.

TRUST ME

Trust you?
Actually, don't.
Are you real?
Fundamentally, you aren't.

Believe you?
Sorry, no.
What part of that was true?
Where did you really go?

Understand you?
Try as we might.
Talking in riddles
Doesn't make it right.

Moving on.
Now so tough.
Easy really:
Enough is enough.

WEATHER UK-STYLE

You can't change the weather.
It's good to have the seasons.
Well, would you really want to?
Do you have a valid reason?

The beauty of the countryside,
The leisure at the beach,
The culture in the cities
All within our reach.

Blown by the wind,
Soaked by the rain –
Even gardens bounce back
When the sun is out again.

The wonders of nature!
Blessed is the UK.
Oh, how lucky we are!
Enjoy it today. ´

YOU ARE MY SUN, SON

The words sound the same:
This comes as no surprise.
Both warm and bright,
And seemingly so wise.

Both turn up together
To brighten a grey day,
Often for no reason.
'Hug' is all they say.

Having a son in your life
The sky is always blue.
There's no better feeling
Unless, of course, you have two.

A golden, shining sun
Will make you get up and out –
A great big tonic,
Of this there is no doubt.

So when they appear
After a long, long while,
Make the most of their presence.
Sure, they'll leave you with a smile.

BIG STAR, LITTLE STARS

Big star,
Big man,
Always saying
Yes you can.

Bless him.

No to that,
Yes to this.
Make a date
He will not miss.

Admire him.

Hulk on legs,
Big smile,
Cheeky chat
On the dial.

Hug him.

Looking after
Little stars
Inside hotels,
Outside bars.

Text him.

Friend to many,
Best dad too,
City-lover,
Never blue.

Adore him.

SMILE

Wear a smile
Inside and out.
Grin and bear it;
Don't give in to doubt.

Rise above the pain;
Float it away.
Dream of somewhere else;
Blank it for today.

It is not for ever,
It's only passing through.
It could have been me –
Sorry that it's you.

For once be looked after.
Let those in the know
Take tests and samples –
Maybe nothing will show.

You are in good hands;
They know more than you.
Stop trying to work out
What's making you blue.

Look out of your window,
Stay warm in the bed,
Get plenty of rest
For body, soul and head.

Conserve your energy
For when you are out.
Everyone is waiting
To see you up and about.

DAY AND NIGHT

Happy days,
Sad nights:
When does the pain go away?

Sad days,
Happy nights:
When does the laughter stay?

Up down,
Down up,
Giggle, laugh and tease.

Cry, howl,
Heartache, sob:
Pain, go away, please.

Too much sorrow,
Not enough fun:
Life is slow to get back.

One day at a time,
Then at night
You are on the right track.

COMING HOME

There's a big smile on their faces:
The children, pets and parents.
This biggest grin is showing
On Mother's, from cheek to cheek.

Coming home at last –
Long time no see.

The house is full of colour;
Happiness shines throughout the rooms,
All clean and fresh and ready
To welcome Father home.

Coming back at last –
Long time no see.

The kids have piles of new hobbies.
The fun will start again
When their elder joins them –
Their loved one so badly missed.

Coming home at last –
Long time no see.

There's nothing left to do:
Just sit and wait.
He'll have plenty of time
To relax and reminisce.

Coming back at last –
Long time no see.

The fridge is overflowing,
His favourite wine is stocked,
His clothes washed and pressed.
Welcome arms await.

Coming home at last –
Long time no see.

They watch the clock's slow hand;
The radio is on.
No more crying and worry –
The strain now nearly gone.

Safely back at last –
Long time no see.

GIFTS

I leave you a gift –
I have nothing else to give.
I am about to die
And you have long to live.

The girls will nurse you
When I am gone.
Give them a call –
It will not be wrong.

I have no money.
I take a final bow
But I leave you my babes –
They are all grown up now.

I'll gain peace knowing
That they will do this
And you'll be safe
When it's me you miss.

They make me so proud
And will make you too.
Look after each other;
Let them look after you.

ALL KINDS OF LOVE

The romantic kind is soft and dewy:
It's candles and meals, Paris and cuddles.
And is it really love?
For it will change.

The family kind is natural and strong,
Its support knows no bounds.
And is it really love
Or just an obligation?

The passionate kind is once in a while,
It's intense and demanding.
And is it really love?
For it will end.

The friendship kind is there and unspoken:
Fun and laughter, singing and dancing.
And is it really love
Or a shadow of you?

The work kind is a joy to be part of:
The challenge and the buzz.
And is it really love
Or filling a void in your life?

The bereavement kind is an ache and pain:
A heart broken in two, someone you miss.
And was it really love?
Of course, but now it has gone.

PRIDE

Who lost?
Who gained?

Who smiled?
Who cried?

Stop and think it through.

You blamed her,
She blamed you.

Enough said,
Enough done.

Stop and think it through.

Stand tall,
Walk on.

Forget it,
Forgive all.

Stop and think it through.

Meet again,
Share a laugh.

Stop
And think.

You're not through.

TOUGH

She is strong,
She is tough,
Though some days weaker –
Then feels rough.

She has many memories
Locked in her mind.
Everyone has been helpful
And so very kind.

She may not see well,
She may have changed her life,
But this is better for her.
Who wants her for his wife?

The grey is becoming darker,
The shadows moving in.
She'll need looking after –
Being ill is no sin.

RUNNING AWAY

Are you running away?
Your family needs you.

You are our star.
Are you coming back?

Running again – but where to?

What will we do?
Don't break our hearts.

We need you here;
Don't you need us?

Running again – but where to?

How will we cope?
You will be free.

The children are so sad.
Is it goodbye?

Running again – but where to?

Can you hear our cries?
They fill the house.

Stop and think.
What is wrong?

Running again – but where to?

Can you turn around?
We'll all be waiting.

No pressures on you.
Is she why you leave us?

Running again? Ah-ha!
So shattered love.

This is a home no more.
Where to now?

Running again.